ENGINEERING CREATIVITY

Or

How to get deliberately
better at being creative

By: Derrick Charbonnet, P. E.

For Kanat

ISBN 979-8-9890141-0-1

Part 1:
WHAT IS THIS BOOK ALL ABOUT?

This is about learning new ways to be creative and a little about some ways about problem solving in general.

Am I qualified to write this? I'm an engineer, what the hell do I know about being creative?

Well, engineers must be very creative. No, we do not create great art or write great literature, but the most challenging part of engineering is solving problems. Every time an engineer is given a task, whether it is to design a rocket to take men to the moon, design a new bridge or building, program a new app, or provide power to a new factory the first thing he or she must do is figure out how. Almost every new thing that you see had an engineer figure out how to design it, the materials it's made of, how to build it, how to package it, and how to get shipped to where you are.

Engineers just might be the most creative people you know.

Even if you are not an engineer, you face challenges every day, at work and at home. Most don't require creative solutions, but some do. If you just can't figure out the solution, maybe following the steps in this book is the path towards that solution.

When I say "problem" here, I am referring to something new that you have to "invent" or something that is not right. In the world of engineering, this could be

- A new device or software to fill a need.
- Fix a failed piece of machinery.
- Something changed in a system and needs to be corrected.
- A process changed and doesn't work as well. This can be any kind of process.

Is this only for engineers? What about the creative arts? Certainly, bringing a work of art to life is a creative process. The process of making that sketch or painting look like that artist wants can be grueling and creative. Taking a lump of clay and turning it into something beautiful requires hard work as well creativity. These works of art also require skill, the skill of hours of practice. Writing is a similar process; it just uses words instead of brush strokes or a potter's wheel. This book is not aimed directly at the creation process; it is aimed at helping you find a solution to a particular problem.

So that means that artists shouldn't use the techniques in here? That's ridiculous. Anyone should use any source of creativity that they can. In fact, the techniques in this book may be able to help the best of artists start a new work, get past a problematic plot point, or fit a unique piece of fabric into a quilt.

One difference between art and engineering is the final product. Beauty is in the eye of the beholder. I may not agree with your definition of a piece of great art. But if a machine works or a repair fixes a problem then we both must agree on that success. It can be poor quality, perhaps not last long, expensive, but with few exceptions if it works: it works; if it doesn't: it doesn't. To be completely fair, the sciences and some of the softer fields such as economics may not be so clear-cut and there *may be* solutions subject to opinion more like a work of art. For what it is worth; I strongly feel creating, engineering, building, testing, and commissioning a custom machine to do a particular task IS a type of sculpture and art. A new machine or piece of software that is simple, elegant, and works really well is a beautiful as any work of art!

"Elegant?" When I am going through this process, I encounter another measure of success: elegance. This is not a measure of beauty directly (though it is a component). It is a measure of how simply, how perfectly, how smoothly, how easily, perhaps how cleverly the solution looks and functions. Elegance has nothing to do with whether the solution actually works or not. Stuffing a sock in a drain to plug it up is not elegant; the way a Rubik's Cube is engineered is. Elegance is a source of satisfaction and pride. You know it when you see it. And when you see it, you can't help yourself, you say "Wow, that's cool." Hopefully, the techniques here will help you find not just working solutions, but great and elegant solutions!!

How about writers and storytellers? Pretty much the same applies, they are just working in a different medium and we hear or read the art instead of seeing it or feeling it. It is a very similar process and with similar problems. The writer can certainly use some of these techniques, as can the seamstress, the glassblower, etc.

"Done Deal" so let's get started, right?

Not so fast. I wrote this book about my experiences. I have spent more than a half-century figuring out how my brain works and how to make it work better. When I was much younger, I attended my share of classes and seminars about time planning, scheduling, project management, design, note taking, etc. Fresh with the new ideas I would take them back to school or work and eagerly use them to make my life better.

Guess what? Most of them didn't work. (But a few did, and I use those every day.)

But they carefully told me how to use them, how they were supposed to work, and how they would help me. But they didn't!! Clearly the person giving the seminar liked the tricks and tips they were teaching. They weren't just some snake oil salesmen peddling worthless ideas. Some people loved the ideas and they did work well. Slowly I realized that my thought processes and quirks are different from the instructors. And I am not some outlier either; many people I knew had the same problem. But everybody usually did find something they could use.

Yes, it seems obvious, we are all different and we all think differently, especially when it comes to creativity. But these instructors either didn't know that or didn't make it clear. I've come up with these techniques over many years of work. They all work for me. Honestly, some of them work much better than others, but they all work. Even though some are only helpful a small percentage of the time, I still use them faithfully because they do give me good ideas. Any tool that helps me will be kept in my mental toolbox. Unless you are a lot like me, the ideas in this book will *not all* work for you. Do not be discouraged, do not "throw the baby out with the bathwater."

My recommendation to you is to read this work carefully, really try the ideas and processes I am presenting. Not just once either, but several times. If there are parts that really don't work for you, then they don't. Don't force them, just like you wouldn't continue using a tool that doesn't work. I would also suggest this: try modifying them to be like the ones that do work. Use the ones that do work and think up some new ones that do!

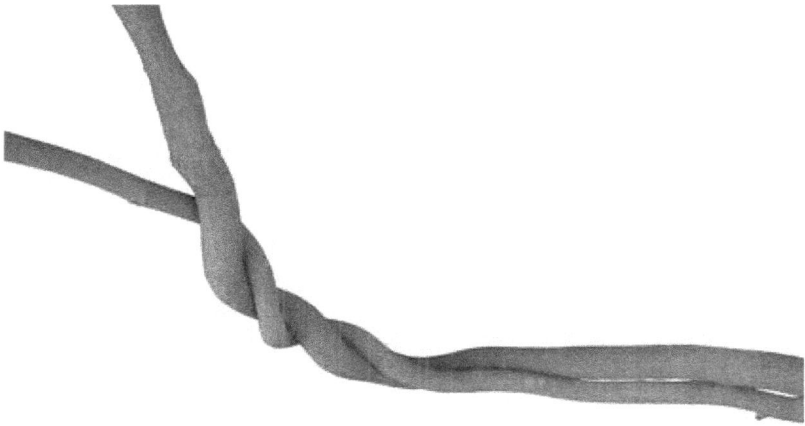

Part 2:
THE PROBLEM

Being creative is all well and good. Artists, writers, potters can create what they want. They can create what looks and feels right to them. If you need a solution for a problem, the first thing that you must do is to ensure that you are actually working on the right problem.

"Of course, I'm working on the right problem, what are you talking about."

If you are learning of the problem from another person, the very first thing that you must be sure of is that you are communicating effectively. There are entire books on this subject, so this book won't go into a lot of detail on the subject. Here are the most important points:

Are you listening to the person? Are you listening with respect? When you are solving a problem, it doesn't matter if you like the person, if they smell funny, if they clearly don't understand what has happened. They have watched it; they probably understand the normal operation of the system better than you ever will. They *will* have information that you need.

If they are asking you to create something new, you must make sure you are creating something that they actually need, and they actually will use.

Does the person understand what is happening? Or just relaying what he sees? Ask questions about what happened. Ask about what used to happen, ask about what goes on before the problem and after?

Look for things that don't make sense. Is the person assuming you know some things about the situation? What happens (ed) before and after the problem event?

Does the person assume something and not even realize he is assuming something? Is his experience coloring his description of the problem? (Hammer and nail problem)

Does this person really understand the problem or is he trying to fix the symptoms (this is a really important question). An example of this situation is that the production supervisor wants you to fix a problem with a molding die, clearly it is a problem with the die because the edges of the product aren't always molding correctly. Is this really a problem with the mold? Is it a problem with the channels feeing the material? Is it a problem with the temperature or pressure of the material? Is there something wrong with the material itself? The symptom, incomplete molding, may have many different and not-so-obvious root causes.

Are you creating something new? There are other, similar concerns. Make sure you understand the parameters and the limits. These can be cost, number of parts, color, weight, size, portability, etc. Make sure you BOTH understand what the person actually wants AND needs and agree to the parameters before you start working.

Another useful thing is to add additional value. As long as we are here and am working on this, is there something more? Are there other problems that have gone on so long that they forgot they are problems? Are there bottlenecks that can be opened? Can I make other parts better? Can it be extended? Can it do something else? Just make sure you don't make anything worse!

Part 3:
CREATIVITY

How does creativity work? Well, if I knew that, I wouldn't have written this. This is written just in case some of the things I do just might help you use your creativity better and more effectively.

Here is what I do know about creativity: It can happen in a flash of insight, it can happen slowly, it can do both? Even the most creative peoples have ways to jog their minds and spark the creativity. The artists I know tend to go through various steps and thoughts to stay creative. Some of the steps are similar to the ones I do and have put in this book. They have ways they look at the world.

You might say: "But I am not creative, how can I do this?"

Everybody is creative, or you wouldn't be human. You just don't think you do creative things for a living like an artist. But, I'll bet lunch that you solve problems in your work or hobby every day. You have done this job for a while and gotten good at it. When you started, you probably weren't very good at it. You didn't know a lot about the things that went on. But as time went by and you got more experienced you got better at the job. You have seen things that help you do your job. I'll guess that you even have solved problems!

What was happening? Practice! Many years ago, I watched a friend sketch something. He is a graphic artist and very good at it. I marveled at his ability. He dismissed my admiration with the comment "I do this every day, that's why I'm good at it. If you did it, you would be too." That offhand comment has stuck with me over the next 3 ½ decades. He is right. Within some limits. If I practiced every day, I would get very good at sketching. However, I don't believe I will ever be as good as him. By the same token, he will probably never be able to create a custom machine as well as I. People are different (yes, we really are) and are better at some things than others.

Does this mean that you shouldn't try? Heck no, try, try again, and keep trying. I am much better at sketching and you can get much better at creativity.

Left Brain vs. Right Brain? There is some very good science that says that this distinction isn't all that it is cracked up to be. However, if you believe that you are "Right Brained" and are not creative, well, you probably won't be creative. You must let yourself try.

Are you going to brilliantly solve the World's problems the first day? Of course not, but you will solve problems creatively and you well do it better as you practice.

Remember when I said we are all different? It's true. Just because I have written a wildly successful website on creativity, it doesn't mean that everything here will work for you. If some of these things don't work for you, DON'T force yourself to do them! Use the ones that do work. Modify the ones that work to work better (maybe even modify the ones that don't!!). You might even discover some new tools that work great for you!

Sometimes you just need to get out of a rut or out of a mental box. These tools are just good for small problems as they are for big problems.

You do have to work at this. It is not magic. Creativity is no different from any other skill.
Practice, practice, practice.

There is one more dimension here. You must give yourself permission to do the things in this book, to be creative, to think differently. Can trying these techniques embarrass you? Yes, you can be embarrassed, but ONLY if you let yourself be embarrassed. Muttering to yourself, waiving you hands in the air while you are looking far away or have your eyes closed can seem a little odd, but when you come up with the answer, then no one will remember the odd part.

Think of this as a set of tools. You would certainly use every tool in your toolbox (or every brush in your paint box, or every pair of scissors in your sewing machine) to fix something. This is just another type of toolbox. Use the tools with the pride of an old-world craftsman. Know in your heart that the people that might make fun of you are small minded and NOT creative!

There is one more thing about these tools. With these tools, please feel free to use them in ways they were not intended. Swing them by the wrong end. Juggle them while they are running. The best part is that you can't hurt yourself. Give it a try!

You work in a team? Well most of these tools work best for an individual. They are engineered to stimulate one's own brain. That doesn't mean teams can't use the tools. Each person in a team can use them. Several people brainstorming can use them. Go through each tool as a team and collect the team's ideas. Try them all as a team, some will work better some will not work so well. It will depend on the people in the team and it will depend on the facilitator. The most important thing is to follow the rules!

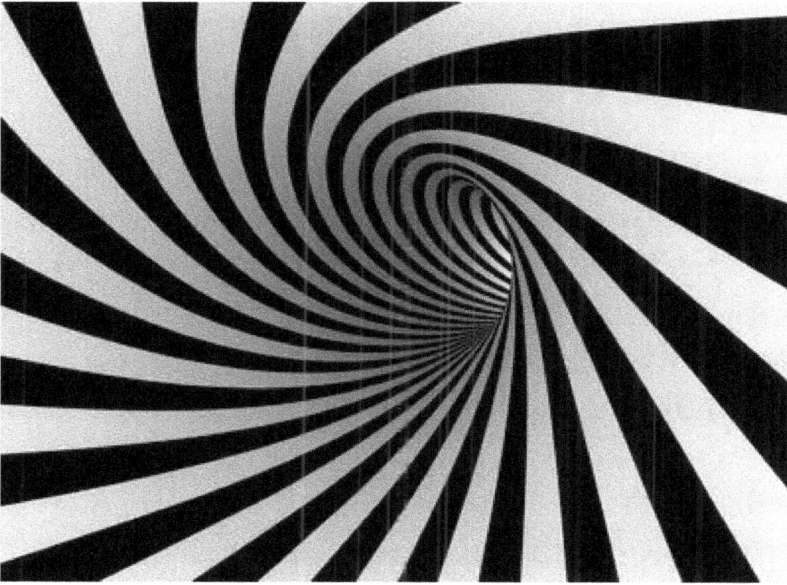

Part 4:
RULES IN A KNIFE FIGHT?!
(with apologies to "Butch Cassidy")

"After all that about using tools anyway you want to, and you are telling me that there are rules after all? I knew it! So much for me developing my creativity."

Not so fast. Yes, there are rules, but these are reverse rules. These rules are there to keep your mind open. Just like communication, there are galaxies of books about brainstorming, so this book won't go into a lot of detail. But I'll give you the important things to remember.

Rule #1: You are the expert on you. You know how you think. Only you can decide what is working and what is not. But you must be honest with yourself.

Rule #2: When you are working through these tools and collecting ideas, DO NOT criticize. There will be plenty of time later to sift out the really good ideas. While you are working through the tools even some goofy and completely wrong ideas may spark better ones. Keep them all until you are done.

Rule #3: Don't try to remember them all. Write them down, scribble them, jot them. Look at the list as you work through the tools. When you decide you are done with the creative part, *then* go through the list and sift it for the best ideas. When you are doing the sifting, give each idea one last thought before you toss it out.

Rule #3A: Ok, some of the best thinking comes in "non-conventional" settings and you can't exactly write them down. When you are being creative in these settings, you will also have to be creative about how you remember and sift through the ideas. Also, as you get better at this, you will get better at the sifting and remembering part, too.

Rule #4: Don't follow the rules! The creative process is almost by definition not a linear process. If you are spending a lot of your mental energy on checking where you are on the process, or making sure you don't miss a tool, or making sure you don't criticize, of carefully write every micro thought that pops up, then you are "following the rules" and you are not "being creative."

I will be honest. Most of the time I don't go through the formal process anymore. But I still do when the problem is intractable, or I just can't seem to come up the right, or a properly elegant answer.

When people are working in groups, it is spectacularly helpful to have a person called a facilitator. There are people trained to do this. A facilitator is sort of like a cross between a coach and referee; the rest of the group is playing the game. The facilitator is the one watching the rules, writing things down, keeping the tempo, and keeping everyone heading towards the right goal. The larger the group the more important it is to have a facilitator.

I have been in meetings and brainstorming sessions with a facilitator trained for that type of meeting. The results were amazing.

Do you have to have a trained facilitator? It would be helpful, but if you don't anyone can take that role. Be careful. The facilitator must be totally non-judgmental, must be able to move the conversation along when it gets stuck or people start repeating themselves. He must make sure that everyone in the group is heard and no one is steamrolled. He can also cajole and help ideas flow sort of like an auctioneer.

Everyone must agree to listen and follow the facilitator lead. People with strong personalities must promise to keep them in check.

Being a facilitator can be a lot of fun, too. You can watch the show (and even toss in some of your own ideas carefully) but you must remember your role and not get caught up in the action.

Part 5:
ARE WE THERE YET DADDY?

Almost. The last recommendation is to make yourself go through these several times before you start judging them too much. Some of them take practice. Some of them may make no sense until you try them a couple of times or maybe tweak them a bit in your mind.

Some of them work better on some kinds of problems, too. Some work worse on some kind of problems. The order doesn't matter. I have presented them in the order that I use.

Give the tools a chance!!!!

The tools come in two major categories.

Thought Tools and Physical Tools. If you are reading this book you are smart enough to figure out what the focus of the two types are so I'm not going to waste ink or electrons explaining. I will use up some ink and some electrons to say that the two kinds of tools are better at different kinds of problems.

Will I give examples? Not really, I don't want poke preconceived notions into YOUR creative process.

All right, saddle up, get out your thinking cap, pen, paper, tablet (paper or computer), a drink, what ever works best. We are off like a herd of turtles!

Part 6:
THOUGHT TOOLS

Thought tools are just that: things that you do in your mind. Some of these you may be able to support by actually holding the thing in your hand and manipulate it while you are thinking about it. But be careful with this. These thought tools are intended to *break down* your "normal" thought patterns about this thing and things in general. If you find yourself sliding back into your normal patterns of thought, stop, back up, and try again.

Remember, the objective of these exercises isn't to just get them done and make your brain work.

It is to get you to look at the different parts and their relationships in totally different ways!

Here they are as a list, you can change the order:

a) Rotate Left
   a. The set of "rotate" tools may take some getting used to. By rotate, I don't just mean to look at the "problem" from the side (though that may be useful to ensure you understand the problem in addition to helping with creativity.)
   b. By "Rotate Left" I mean to take each part of the problem and mentally rotate that part more or less ¼ of a turn to the left in your mind. Then make what ever is the problem happen. Imagine what happens.
   c. Of course, it will probably be silly. The candy bars will fall on the floor, or you will see the side of the box on the advertisement. But maybe if you rotated the candy bar instead of the conveyor. Hmmmmmm. Even the things that don't make sense just might help you visualize a clever new solution.
   d. Rotate to the left the entire area or parts, or machinery around the problem, what is happening around it? What is happening to things that are coming or going into that area?

b) Rotate Right
   a. Do the same thing but the other direction.
   b. Yes, this may really matter. Most things are not symmetrical enough to make this the same as rotating left.

c) Rotate ½ way around.
   a. Yep, do the same thing as before but take each part and the whole and rotate it until you "see" the back (180 degrees).
   b. This is actually two parts. You should try rotating each part and the whole 180 degrees to the left and then again, from the start, rotate each 180 degrees to the right.
   c. You might even try rotating each part all the way around just to "see" what happens. The end point won't teach you much because it is the same as the start. But something clever may pop up while you are doing it.

d) Rotate Up
   a. Yep, the same thing. Take each part and rotate it up ¼ of the way. The take the whole area and rotate it up.
e) Rotate Down
   a. Take each part and the whole, rotate down.
f) Rotate ½ way up and down.
   a. This one is also two parts. You want to rotate the problem 180 degrees but rotate it up 180 degrees and then down 180 degrees.
g) Turn it over
   a. Here's where it gets interesting. This is not just a variation of the rotation test.
   b. This one may take some getting used to. Try to visualize this as though you were watching Claymation or a cartoon.
   c. Take the middle top of the thing, mentally push the top down through the middle until it is at the bottom. Move the bits around a bit. Any ideas?
   d. Reverse that. Take the original bottom and push it through the top.
   e. Do this with each of the four sides.

h) Turn it inside out.
   a. Pick one of the last 4 tests
   b. Take that part you pushed through and continue, moving all of the bits with it.
   c. Move all the parts until it is inside out.
   d. This one can be very hard to imagine, or it can be easy, depending on the actual thing you are working with. Just remember, the objective isn't to successfully make the thing inside out. *It is to make you think about the parts in a different way.*
   e. So as long as this process has gotten some of your gray matter going, you have indeed achieved success.

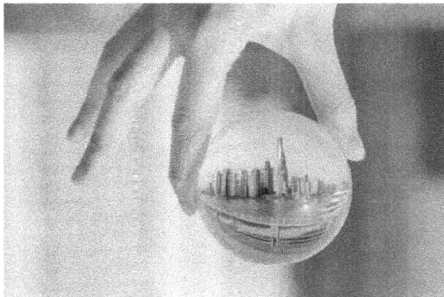

i) Now for something completely different:
   a. Make it huge!
   b. How do the parts change? How to they fit with the world? Is it easier to see some inside part? Could you fit something else in there?
   c. Make it tiny!
   d. How do the parts change? How do they fit with the world? Have some parts vanished? Can you put it in something?

j) What else does something like this or look like this?
  a. An animal?
      i. Dog
      ii. Cat
      iii. Mouse
      iv. Snake
      v. Giraffe
      vi. Buffalo
      vii. Horse
      viii. Mouse
      ix. I think you get the idea here. Run through an imaginary zoo. Do any of the animals give you any ideas?
  b. A vegetable?
      i. Tree
      ii. Bush
      iii. Grass
      iv. Mold
      v. Flower
      vi. Vine
      vii. Seaweed
      viii. Run through an imaginary world looking at plants you have seen.
  c. A mineral?
      i. Stone
      ii. Chalk
      iii. Mud
      iv. Crystal
      v. Glass
      vi. Sand

vii. Steel
viii. Brass
  ix. Mercury
   x. Run through a museum

d. How about any other machine you have seen?
     i. A mixer
    ii. A toy car
   iii. A pair of scissors
    iv. A paper clip
     v. A spinning wheel
    vi. A nut and bolt
   vii. A revolver
  viii. An electric toothbrush
    ix. Run through a department store, a hardware store, an antique store.

k) Try something ridiculous. Did I mention that the objective is *to make you think about the parts in different ways?*
    a. This may depend on what you are working with
    b. Have an elephant step on it
    c. Let Picasso have a go at it and let it sag
    d. Wring it out like a wet towel.

These are my mental tests. Feel free to add, modify, remove, play.

**Remember the measure of success is
new and different ideas**

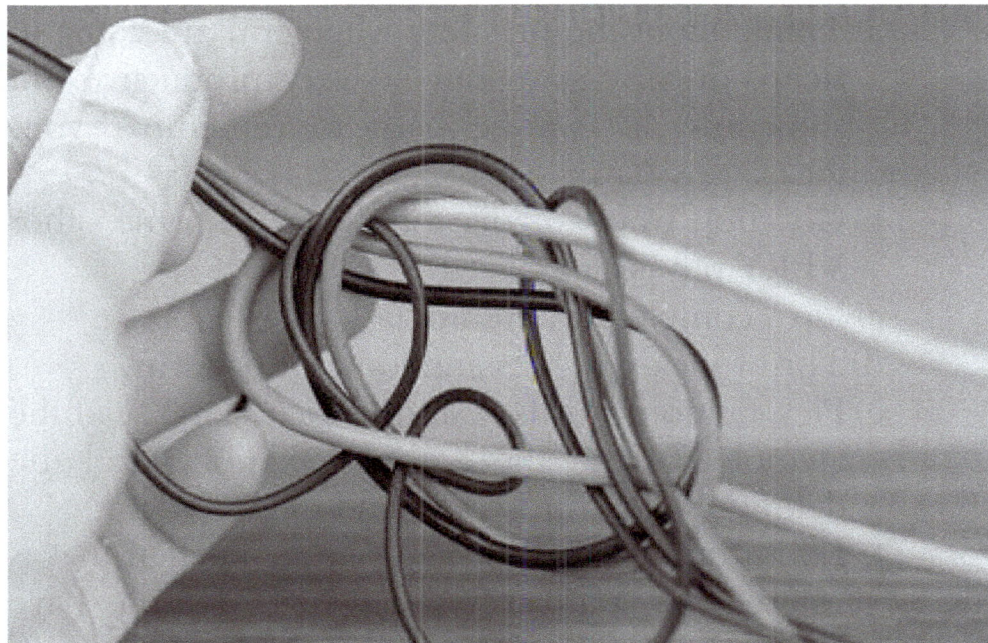

Part 7:
PHYSICAL TOOLS

These tools are intended to use a physical motion or position to break your thinking patterns. Please be careful. Don't hurt yourself but do think about your problem while you are doing these things, sort of in the back of your head. You may want to have some paper close to take notes.

a) Think about the problem when you are going to sleep, dreamy state can be very productive but sometimes it can be hard to remember your ideas.
b) Go chop wood or dig a hole or do some other **VERY** physical task.
c) Do a completely different task.
d) Throw pick-up sticks and look for patterns.
e) Pick random words from the dictionary; read the etymology, read the entire definition, read the definition of a word you found there.
f) Look through that drawer in your kitchen that is where you put everything that doesn't have another place. Can you use any of those shapes?
g) Grab two things that don't belong together, hold them together and make them move about. These can resemble your problem, or they can be very different, of both!
h) Go to Wikipedia (give them a donation so your conscience is clear). Pick a like from the front page. Glance through that article and look at the pictures. Pick a link in that article, pick a like there; follow a rabbit from one link to another,
i) Do something that involves motion. Any new patterns?
j) Do some routine task in a completely different way

Part 8:
THE LAST TEST

Mentally grab a blank sheet of paper: draw a brand-new solution, draw several.

Grab a real sheet of paper and doodle some new solutions.

This is not only the end of the brainstorming part of the solution; but it is the start of the actual solution.

Just remember, this process can be repeated, every time you run into a stumbling block. Every time you just are not happy with what you have.

Part 9:
SOME MORE RULES

✓ Don't stop at the first good answer.
✓ Don't run off with the first idea, there may be better ones.
✓ Go through the whole process, on the rare occasion when the first idea is the best, other ideas may improve it.
✓ Compare your answers and ideas with each other; can you use one to make another one better?
✓ Sometimes you just know there is still a better idea out there.
  ○ Keep trying, up to a point
✓ Sometimes you just go with what you have.

Part 10:
THE THRILL OF VICTORY

You will know when it works. You will come up with THE answer. That perfect elegant answer, just a few tweaks to finish it.

Wow, there is nothing better (almost).

Thanks for reading this bit of my imagined wisdom. I truly hope it helps!
Derrick Charbonnet

If you are interested in discussing this more, you can find me. I have left a pretty broad trail in life.

www.ingramcontent.com/pod-product-compliance
Lightning Source LLC
Chambersburg PA
CBHW060647030426
42337CB00018B/3481